EYES OF THE HEALER

EYES OF THE HEALER

NELOFAR CURRIMBHOY

BLOOMSBURY
NEW DELHI • LONDON • OXFORD • NEW YORK • SYDNEY

BLOOMSBURY INDIA
Bloomsbury Publishing India Pvt. Ltd
Second Floor, LSC Building No. 4, DDA Complex
Pocket C – 6 & 7, Vasant Kunj
New Delhi 110070

BLOOMSBURY, BLOOMSBURY INDIA and the Diana logo are trademarks of Bloomsbury Publishing Plc

First published in India 2017
This paperback edition published 2023

ISBN: 978-93-56403-09-3
2 4 6 8 10 9 7 5 3 1

Printed and bound in India

To, Poets
Poetry and it's Believers

PRAISE FOR THE AUTHOR

'UNPUTDOWNABLE! A fascinating read for all who dare to dream.'

– *The Times of India*

'Nelofar Currimbhoy has done an outstanding job! The ease...with which she takes her readers along on an awe-inspiring journey, is noteworthy.'

– *The Tribune*

'Absolutely riveting. Written by Nelofar Currimbhoy, Husain's daughter, this book (*Flame*) is an exceptionally insightful biography, an open book on her life.'

– *Femina*

'Crisp, Fast Paced...we now have a new author in the form of Currimbhoy.'

– *The Sunday Pioneer*

'*Flame* can inspire many to turn adversity into success.'

– *Hindustan Times*

She (Currimbhoy) studs her narrative with not only the enthusiasm of one who has watched this incredible story unfold but also the warmth of one who has loved unconditionally.

– *IBN Live*

'*Flame* is interspersed with witty lines and interesting anecdotes.'

– *Atelier*

'Currimbhoy provides a fascinating insight into the personal and professional life of this remarkable woman.'

– *Sahara Times*

'A riveting narrative...'

– *Mumbai Mirror*

CONTENTS

MY JOURNEY WITH THE HEALER...

Nothing I have written or will ever write, can mean more to me than Eyes of the Healer. When I read the Healer today, it feels like a 'prayer' to the creativity within. I wrote the first ten verses in the still of the night with an overused pencil in a small diary which I kept on my bed side table for inspirational moments such as this. The next day I wrote some more and this went on till the diaries moved to my brand new computer. By now the character of Govinda was simply my soul connect. His search for the infinity, his passion his love, his Maya came to life as only inspired writing can.

It is wondrous to create a character and then see him take a life of his own. The narrative propels him forward, things happen, he evolves, matures, perhaps ages; he moves within his time and space and finally your writing becomes a response to the one your pen created.

As an author I would say, there are two kinds of writing—the stories that a writer plans and carefully creates to publish. He thinks of the reader's response, the reaction; a sense of being visible to the world, shadows that work and then there is something he may write purely for his soul to, find its way to its most beautiful fantasies; in my case it was about mystical fantasies. Healer was never planned for publication. It was quite simply my soul pouring and I sense in it a purity I may never find again.

I believe in the power of poetry and its potential more than ever today. In an environment where reading habits are changing constantly, an Ode to a Grecian Urn by John Keats can be as satisfying as a novel. Poetry, as lyrics set to music in the voice of Leonard Cohen or the Nobel Prize-winning Bob Dylan will always have the strongest impact on our lives.

The amazing quality of poetry is that it is not just read like all other literature but it is equally heard. It can be appreciated even by someone who cannot read. The concept of poetry reportedly dates back to pre-literacy times when rhythm became a mechanism to remember lines jotted in the mind. Poetry is all around us, it is an intrinsic part of our lives. In miniscule forms it appears in jingles on your TV ads, greeting cards, musicians and vocalists all rely on the beautiful amalgam of words and tunes. I also believe that poetry softens the tonality of your language and I would go to the extent of saying that it influences the way you live your lives. I don't think the Healer could have been what it is if it were not written in verse.

So as I send my Healer out to the world I would say to you dear reader, I do so with a prayer and the hope that it touches your hearts and minds, that it changes your world simply by the way you look at it.

April, 2017 **Nelofar Currimbhoy**

New Delhi

1

SEEKER

Crimson robes and holy beads,
Anointed waters and Oakwood seeds,
Temple bells, lilting echoes,
The gentle rustling of sacred leaves;
A divine dance –
Languidly swaying Banyan trees.

Whistling winds, lyrical, mystical,
Soft serenading nightingale,
Her hypnotic tune she did sing;
'Partners tonight, Plotters tonight'
– In Nature's irresistible conspiracy.

Just seventeen,
Govinda, young full-blooded man,
Slim, sinewy, almost feline,
Skin shone, a molten brown,
Testimony to the hours spent,
Meditating under the firmament.
Dark misty eyes,

Seeped in learnings,
Intoxicating wine,
Mind in orbit,
A butterfly
Weightless, free,
A citadel of perfect harmony.
Of matter and dreams,
Of soul and form,
Treading the unseen line,
Where earth and the hemisphere divide.

Resisting all pressures
On soul and psyche,
A moment's hesitation –
'Is this the oasis of my dreams?'
He looks away for fear of defeat,
Conquering surging uncertainties.
Just one step,
Just one more step,
One shining, glowing step,
To the doors of
Ethereal sanctuary.
Heavy feet, cracking through gravity,

He looks heavenwards and feels
The strength
Of his prayers.
If there is a God,
He would be halfway there.
And then he takes the final flight,
'A vow of silence!'
Echoes the voice of the head priest
Govinda swears never to speak.

Draped in a garment of austerity
The swirling fabric, a warm flame
Engulfing his earthly human body–
Yet that strange dichotomy,
Freeing his mind of worldly needs,
Like a dove soaring to unknown heights,
Rising to the final spirituality,
His eyes like burning embers glow,
Perched on the precipice
Of Divinity.

'Close them,'
A tone of authority

'Gaze through your soul,
And you shall walk
Through the hallowed
Doorways of Eternity.'

So with eyes shut earnestly,
He sat for ten utopian years,
Under the swaying Banyan trees;
Long, raven tresses,
Billowing in the morning breeze,
Fingers rotating the sacred beads,
Gods churning the cosmic wheels
Exposed to the elements,
Oblivious of the searing heat,
Until the millionth devotee,
Had touched his glowing feet.

2

WANDERER

Memories of a fading life,
All immersed in the depths of time
Yet like a whirlpool rising in his mind,
Swirling through her lovely womb,
Echoes of his mother's voice:
'Govinda! Govinda!' she did call,
'My hapless child, why in the wilds
Do you roam
Like a wounded antelope?
What pain is it you hide?
Sit by me and bare your soul.'

'Oh, Mother, you are everything to me,'
He gently bends to touch her feet;
'You are my creator, the only god
That I can see.
Yet within me, there is a constant call
From the mountains,
And far beyond,
My soul leaves my body each night,

Across timeless realms it takes flight.'
He looks away; deep mystic eyes.
'This body, Ma, is a prison,
A camouflaged confine,
This face a masked disguise,
I am the captor of my soul,
Where I walk, entrapped,
It must follow.
I wonder if it longs to be set free,
I wonder what its realms may be.
But for today,
I am the mentor of my soul
And I must lead it to where it longs to go.'

Alarmed, she holds him tight
As he speaks without respite:
'Many worlds do lie
Between here and the stars,
Between this earth and the skies;
A million energies
Singeing flames,
Unhindered fires
This is not the only order,

Millions more wait at its drifting borders,
Where the mind alone must travel,
And leave the body behind.'

She slips away,
While he speaks on,
An urgency in her quickening gait,
Windblown hair and restless veil.
At the holy river she keenly waits,
And watches her husband pull down the sails.
His aging arms drag splintered oars,
On a journey that has no shore,
And in that fading, exhausted state,
He sails the river for all his days.
Where does he reach?
Are all those miles just in vain?
She fleetingly feels his numbing pain.

In his dreams
He sailed high seas,
Fought with pirates,
Touched unseen lands;
Egypt, Turkey, Arabian sands,

Forbidden grapes from silken hands,
Sailors' nights and reveling gangs.

The creaking boat groans day's end,
Worn out traveler, faithful friend,
Scraping clay on mud-drenched banks.
'You come to me, my lovely wife!'
His gentle face breaks into a smile,
'Sit by me, and talk a while.'

'Our son,' she cries, 'is in a spell,
The gods do call him, I can tell,
What should we do to keep him home?
I cannot think of us alone.'

The wise old man calmly hears,
One by one,
Each precious
Word he sears:
His eyes moist, stare at her,
The river trapped, within forever,
Face etched, engraved with lines,
Like rising waves and dipping tides.

Go to the village whore,' he says
'Tell her I'll give her my boat, and more
If she can use her allure,
To bring back Govinda to our door.'

3

TEMPTATION

The night is hot and moist,
Echoes of bangles,
Hushed footsteps, bells on ankles,
Reveling in the ritual's delights,
Jhumki sways gently to the night,
Moonbeams gilding her body,
Soft and light.

Govinda stares in surprise,
Temptation, lust, ebbing desires –
'Should I surrender to the sensations of life?
Embrace this sweet respite,
Is this part of this order,
This unleashed fire?'

Jhumki, moves in measured steps,
Gingerly brushes his winged chest,
His raven tresses on soft shoulders rest,
Sweet heady fragrance; her enticing breath,
Struggling, resisting her final crest,

Sinewy body in restive turmoil,
Pulling away, he gently recoils.

Eyes ignite, denying defeat,
Unveils her body to her feet,
Skilful seductress,
She slithers beside,
Weaving her form –
Half woman, half serpentine.
Her movements a masterly craft,
Soft meditative, a mesmerising art.
Reaching beyond yet holding back;
Searching, seeking
Playfully retreating
Passion flowing then softly receding,
Winning;
Watching resolutions
Breaking.

4

PHANTHOM

Sun-kissed valley,
Soft wayward breeze,
Freshly sown barley in virgin fields,
Yesterday lies
Engulfed by
Eternity.

Part wakeful,
Part in spellbound sleep,
Lips languid, tracing passion's dreams,
Skin luminous –
The afterglow of ecstasy.

Like a peacock
Unfurling its exquisite trail,
Jhumki stretches,
Rolls her eyes, in triumph smiles,
'A lion-tamer am I
A conqueror of men,'
She whispers gleefully.

'And now I own the village boat,
And will sail on it, like a queen.'

Long, ringed fingers seek to her side
The hollow where he slept;
Stares gaping –
Just an empty depth.
Gone! Like shifting light
Phantom of a surreal night,
Eluding the grip of worldly life.

She knows
He would not look back,
Nor fall again
In her mesmeric trap,
Or dwell on her sensuous charms,
Her deeper realms,
Her infinite powers
– That fought the Gods for one endless night,
And held them back
From their coveted prize.

Was he a man or an ethereal form?
His body an apparition,

A receding mirage,
A divine gift,
She decides.
Then softly smiles
A prayer for him:
'Young restless man in
quest of God,
May you find him,
when you reach his door.'

5

THE RISING

Misty visions of another life,
Smoldering, melting,
Fading away, his fists held tight,
Conquering the remains of past lives.

Now behold this breath-taking sight:
Like a meteor shooting through the night,
Journeys of that restless mind,
Soaring eagle, wings taut, sublime,
Surging to the final rise,
Ascending the seven stages
Of Divinity.
Behold the birth of a greater energy.

Fires dying and some gone wild,
Stars, moons and travelling lights,
His body turns pale and cold,
Lifeless and still, yet his head,
Wears a cupola of gold.
It has happened!'

Cries the voice of the head priest,
'Govinda has found Divinity.'

The word spread wide,
The word spread strong,
In the monastery of Arna,
A God is born,
And so they throng –
Rows of humanity,
Swaying lines, serpentine long
Worshippers at the doors of God –
Partners in the bond of pain,
Believers in the power of faith.

A woman draped in a pure white veil,
Wearing her widowhood like a restless sail.
Etched pain on her brutalized back shone,
Her body, her carved tomb stone,
Torn drapes on a battered wife,
Covering herself with her shredded pride,
A leper with oozing wounds,
His fingers stubbed like worn-out spoons,
Crying babies on tired breasts,

Clinging to their mothers,
Like birds in warm nests,
A nubile face marred by pearly boils,
Warring diseases, their triumphant spoils,
A soldier bearing warm emblem-shaped gashes,
His dreams of glory in smoldering ashes,
And just for one glance,
This lonely soul,
Miles behind the hungry droves,
Walking like a tired troll,
His body dragged on broken pegs,
The man they called, 'Poor Wooden-Legs'.

Anxiety grows,
Yet patience stays,
Until finally
Govinda's body sways.
Silence strikes, as faith and prayer
Pave the way,
And so they finally rise,
Those mystical powerful,
Life-affirming eyes.

The crowds rise
And swarm to see,
'The Eyes of the Healer';
And seek their spiritual energy.
Each ailing one,
Blessed with his gaze,
Of eyes filled with seething cosmic rays,
Caressing disease,
Soothing pain,
Soaking tears,
Tracing each atom, each single grain.

Women smile; men rejoice,
The widow smiles, draped in relief,
Pain dissolves like sand,
Deep oceans of peace;
Tears sinking into the depths of his eyes,
Joy, laughter,
Fading cries.

In this ecstatic pantomime,
Govinda ceases to sense the drift of time,
Crust of bread held out to him,

Drops of water on flaking lips,
Fountainhead of generosity,
His body a temple, His body a shrine,
His life force a new religiosity.

His Healing Eyes finally waver,
Eclipsed of intensity,
Faint breath and fading energies
Drawing from parched reservoirs,
'One more sufferer, O Lord, let me heal!'

Give him respite!'
Calls the head priest,
Govinda feels his senses retreat,
Eyes shut
In deep meditative repose,
Journeys past hemispheres,
Fading shore-lines
In quest of celestial mysteries
To heal once more,
Disease pain, its miseries.

6

SURRENDER

Cartwheels of day and night
Cosmic play of dark and light
Earth a charmed Rumi dancer
Gently twirls,
Swooning, spinning
Hypnotically driven,
Circling the ring of undying reason,
Questioning the mystery of her existence.
Seeking divine enlightenment;
For eternal Spring to her changing seasons.

On her thousandth revolution;
Govinda repeated
The golden Mantra,
Releasing his tangible soul
Surrendering it to the universe,
Swatantra.
The stars had moved
To mysterious positions;
Patterns of life,

In floating formations,
The air was warm,
With intangible expectation,
Beads of sweat,
Brow moist with sudden perspiration,
Govinda sensed an inexplicable vibration,
Helpless under the force of that sensation,
Govinda opened his eyes.

Dazzling light, a glowing apparition,
An ethereal beauty, draped in red,
Demure, nubile, the Raja's young bride,
Lips curved; innocence unchecked,
Gentle smile; bows out stretched,
Slender neck, ancestral jewels bedecked,
Sparkling diamonds, sapphires, emeralds,
Frail wrists bonded in bridal bangles,
Dainty feet chained in intricate anklets,
Soft, silken, wind-rippled hair, and
Sun-kissed hands –
A woman from an alien land.

And while the faithful wait,
In long winding lines,

Men, women, the ailing child
Govinda gazes mesmerized,
Spellbound by the woman
By his side.
Unwittingly,
She had seized
The Healer's Eyes.

Restive hordes in despair
Screams of pain rent the air,
His senses encased within her soul,
In a trance, beyond control.
Lips sealed,
His eyes, in visions of life, did speak:
'My soul is a lonely hunter,
That traversed the stars in wonder,
From where passion does flow
But through the echoes of thunder,
From that unseen sanctum,
Where love enshrouds the soul,
Through the eternal path,
To surrender,
From where the mirage of my existence,
Will blend into yours forever.'

Human once more,
For a fleeting moment,
The thoughts that flowed,
They touched her soul,
And he could sense her reply.
Bonds of undying love were kept,
Lit up her eyes, in the flaming lamplight,
Flecks of amber crushed ignite,
And forever more; since that fateful day,
She came each melting orange dusk,
Unaware; entrapped,
To sit and gaze into his eyes,
And reaffirm her unspoken love,
No demands—no persuasions,
Just quiet acceptance,
His sight her salvation.

Chained within their boundaries,
Mystical lovers,
Sitting across an invisible line,
Sensing love, in its sublimity
Love, the sages have said, was blind,
But this enchanted love,

Was pure, serene ethereal,
With no words to define.

The hungry droves shiver in dismay,
Faith like wax melts away,
Hope flickers like a dying flame,
Panic, confusion,
Screams and prayers –
Worn out, disillusioned,
Once again,
In that chaotic disarray,
Waiting still was 'Poor Wooden-Legs',
His eyes grew red in despair
Shaking in angry jolts
Holding up his glistening knife
Tearing through his legless strife.

Now look!
Watch this unholy sight,
If your eyes can bear this plight;
Bonded by their agonies,
Rejected by earthly borders,
Waiting at new boundaries,

Turning away
From the Stupa of faith,
Lost, directionless,
Orphaned by their healer,
Like a procession of floating ghosts,
They strayed away,
The weary hordes.

Incense burning,
Tobacco singeing,
Souls scorching,
Sweating bodies,
Dust clouds rising
Wounds bleeding,
Devils smiling,
Aromas mingling,
Gods reclining,
Pain shining.

7

CAPTIVES

Canopy of woven flowers encased,
Ancient bridal bed, silver inlaid,
She lay in her gilded cage,
Draped in soft silken sheets,
Beautiful Maya, eyes serene.
Through wafts of incense smoke,
She sees,
Floating images in merging scenes,
Drifting lands in fluid tracks,
Melting faces in candle wax.

The Raja admires his exquisite queen,
His restless breath against her skin,
Firm hands through her body slide,
Thoughts in turmoil, her mind does spin,
Soft shaking voice cleaves the night in half,
The palace walls collapse like a pack of cards:
'My lord, if you want to live with me,
My body can never belong to thee,
For I have taken a holy vow,

And though I shall serve your every need,
Forgive me this—my destiny.'

His hands shaking in retreat,
The Raja searches her eyes,
Flickering flames of fire-light,
Stunned as he realized,
That she was lost,
To some glorious spell,
Between two worlds,
Transcending to Nirvana,
Where monks,
And priests,
And angels dwell.

The sun rose hesitantly
The way her eyes opened,
Reluctantly.
Maya, guileless bride of one endless night
Her hands red with henna shone,
Intricate patterns of days unknown,
Hair perfumed with jasmine flowers,
Still fragrant

Sweet dew
Of valleys afar.

'Dulhan Rani sleeps till now,'
Sniggers of a whispered voice,
Muffled sounds,
The ceaseless giggling of court boys;
Stamping of heavy feet,
As the Raja moves away to leave
Maya,
Her gaze guiltless
Free,
Esoteric innocence;
Like running brooks, flowing clear
Expression
Devoid of mortal fear.
Confounded, the Raja turns back,
By an inexplicable divine order.
Moving like a shadow,
Fortitude giving way to anger,
A player in heavenly games
And celestial plans.

8

PLAYER

Her body with gifted gold did glitter,
Sequenced drapes of chiffon
Blatantly a-shimmer.
'I will follow the Rani where she may go,
And if she does have a lover,
I swear,
In the name of the Lord of the Thousandth Sun,
He will lie dead at your door.'
Her palm made heavy with silver coins,
Jhumki,
The thousandth courtesan of exotic dreams,
Humbled by the royal presence,
Soft footed, in reverence,
Steps back, face forward, bent,
As into the blanket of night,
Did her swaying form merge.

Ego injured, honour at stake,
The Raja then mounted his faithful steed,
Ancestral sword held, unsheathed,

Bugle calls,
From ramparts of palace walls
An army of soldiers he did lead.
Yearning for the battle field,
Its tragic yet spellbinding din,
To fight a war that he could win.

9

COSMIC CLAY

The ancient seat of learning, Arna,
Where the sun resists setting,
It burns, it smolders,
It suffers,
At last it melts.
Where sunrise is not merely for light,
But each morning an awakening,
A Luminescence,
An insight.

A star-ship waiting at unknown borders,
Sacred halfway home to a greater order,
Shelter of prophets,
Creator of mystical minds,
Look, seek and be enshrined,
Hold your breath; let your senses ignite,
Spellbound are you,
By this mystifying sight.

The ancient seat of learning, Arna,
Through amber glow rising;

Clouds ascending, cascading,
Anointing, caressing,
Winds whispering, playfully billowing,
Stretching steeples, watch them rise,
Yearning to touch sacred skies,
Like the arms of holy men,
Reaching for blessings divine.
Columns in rows,
Guards in stone,
Stand vigil
On moonless nights.
Forever loyal, frozen,
Patient and still.
Rosewood carvings,
Smiling Buddhas,
Grinning cynically at Time.

The ancient seat of learning, Arna,
Coming to life.
Do you hear them now?
Whispering through the night,
The ghosts of dead men,
Chanting without respite,

Shadows moving to and fro,
With no origin.
Whispering words of wisdom,
Omens, forebodings,
Cosmic ministrations,
Mysterious tremors,
Inexplicable vibrations,
The magnificent energies of the Stupa,
Coming to life.

The sacred walls of Arna,
Breathing from each pore,
Inhaling, holding,
Softly exhaling,
Energies surging,
Moving, waiting, shifting,
The dance of Creation struggling,
Atoms waltzing,
Rising, falling,
Halting, aching, battling,
Life forms evolving, seeking
Finally,
Breathing.

Mud and mortar, sand and grain,
Or perhaps fragments of men
Who died not in vain,
But nourished the earth
With the atoms of their remains
Life preserved, remolded,
Sustained,
And over a million years, took different
Forms and shapes,
In the potter's wheel, palpable clay;
All matter returns to Earth,
Generous Mother,
To nourish her warm womb,
Hold her to the eternal promise
Of rebirth.

So hear them tonight,
The living walls of Arna,
Touch them, feel them,
Sense their strife!

'Govinda, Govinda,'
A million voices beg,

'Govinda, Govinda!'
Echoes reverberate,
'Heal, heal,
Govinda, come out of this spell!'

10

PERHAPS GOD

Behold him
As he breaks through a sliver of light,
Ancient Reincarnate,
Chiseled by the sands of time,
A statue in spotless white,
Dharam, the ageless priest of Arna.
Shoulders spread wide,
A falcon's strong wings,
In spirited flight.

Deep piercing eyes,
Gleaning, learning, seeking
His senses,
The universe internalized,
His form,
Magnificence personified,
Compelling image of,
Truth, folklore and fantasy.
Great orator from another time,
Hear him and be mystified,

He weaves his words like a mesh;
Imagery, vision, thoughts
In exquisite verbal tapestry
Connect.

His followers swoon,
They catch their breath.
An ocean of learning;
Confluence of rivers,
Where deep wisdom met
Fierce intellect.

'Warm your soul on a cold winter's day,
Men of insatiable earthly desires,
Until your soul and mind are enriched,
And you shine like a beacon,
Through the firmament.
Walk through this cloud of knowledge,
And with its mist be drenched.'

The devotees weep in gratitude,
Pursuers of an elusive God,
Tracking his fading footsteps, to Arna's doors

He stares at them– tired and spent,
Empty of all thoughts,
But this night would have no end,
As head priest of Arna,
He suffered, he wondered, he agonized,
His mind transfixed on the Healer's eyes.

Walking in quick, anxious strides,
Robes flowing down his awesome height
Embracing each holy priest, as he arrived,
Candles flickering, beads rotating,
Lips chanting, chanting-chanting,
Wheels churning, forever turning,
Planets swirling, stars burning,
Prayers repeating, repeating,
Repeating,
Shadows fading, fading,
Deep into the night.

Congregation of monks and priests,
Tomorrow's Gods, thinkers,
Wise men indeed,
'Govinda, Govinda,'

They rhythmically called.
A million moons later,
A Mahatma was born
Govinda, you were the chosen one.

Suggestions, protons, mantras talismans,
Rolls of yellow flaking, scriptures read,
Is there a way, to crack this spell,
Tolling Arna's ancient bells,
Calling on their unknown strengths,
And as Govinda sat beyond mortal reach,
The greatest of men, did humbly retreat,
And at the doors of Arna,
Accept defeat.

Dharma worn out, lay as his body slept,
Mind in a chasm, entering another realm.
Moist brow and beads of sweat,
A restless night of visions and sounds,
Gods, angels, spirits did abound,
'Bring him his mother!'
A voice in his dreams.

Mystic paths and invisible guides.
Kamla gazed into her son's eyes
With a sense that sight denies,
Ravaged by time,
Silver-haired, old and blind
Following the scent of her child
Evoking the forces a mother's
Womb enshrined.
'Ma!' said Govinda.
Like a wounded bird,
Breaking his silence for that invincible word
That encompassed all creation,
Celestial spaces,
The universe.

'Govinda, my son, I am blind,
Bring back your powers, give me my eyes.'

Shaking fingers trace his face,
Between his brows they touch the space,
Memories of his younger days,
Govinda's body begins to swoon,
Fire within, sun-scorched high noon,

Moist brow beaded with sweat,
He heaved for breath,
Struggling for his vanquished strength,
Rising through the infinite well,
He cried, he groaned, to break the spell,
Still mesmerized, one more look,
At his mother's pain,
Govinda would his powers regain.

But Kamla could not bear his screams,
Reaching out she bid him peace,
A mother voice, a soothing balm,
A soft embrace, healing calm.

'Beautiful son, I see you beyond sight,
The Gods and Saints appear in your light,'
For one final touch her hand on his face,
Feeling her child like a sacred brail,
Then pulling away she let herself flee,
'The spiritual path is your destiny.
My gifted one, I bless your infinite journey.'

11

ECHO

Wait! Do you hear that voice?
Deep commanding resonance,
Dharma stood on the hillside,
His feet on jagged rocks astride:
'I may not have the Healer's eyes,
But heed my wisdom, my advice.

Hold my words like Rudraksh beads,
Turn them around like endless wheels,
The fire-walker feels no sting,
What the mind rejects does not exist
Pain hurts, when the senses accept.
Raging fires lie extinguished
Flames turn to icicles thin,
Nurture not your pain,
Set it free.
Watch it, as it leaves your mortal body,
Released into infinite space,
Eternity.

At the Stupa of Arna you bend your head,
The temple you seek is within yourself,
Seek and you will find,
The voice of God in you entwined.

Say out Loud:
This body I cleanse,
I wash it of hate,
Of regret remorse,
I forgive I embrace,
I remember only the gentlest days.
Take into my soul a fresh beginning,
Like mountain kissed air
I breath in positivity, I breath out negativity
On the footsteps of God's plan
Just as I take in oxygen and spill out carbon,
I live, I seek,
I draw the light of the Universe in me.

Seek not the medicine man,
Nor the sick homes,
Go instead to where life heals life,
Where the air is fresh, the waters pure,

Where the light of a million stars falls on you,
And sunlight sinks into the earth
healing every atom on its unhindered path.

And tire not your soul in changing others
Be at peace,
In conflict the joy of life does cease.
There is no right and there is no wrong.
What you argue for is
your right against another's right
And non can judge which is greater,
For you see the world through your window
and he from another,
and from both the view is perfect,
Yet never the same.

As for happiness, that elusive bird of heaven,
Seek that bliss not for yourself but for those nearest,
And the joy given will touch your life,
Bless your world and light your path,
For you are not an Island and your happiness
Seeks you in your ring of love.

And regret not if your wealth is less
and envy not your friends with riches,
For what can be bought is of no value,
The sun the moon, the embrace of love,
The smile on a child's face,
have no price.

Seek not more till you have received,
Blessings given still wait, gathering rust,
To seek is your inherent lust,
Return home, throw open your vaults,
Unwrapped gifts, unnoticed bliss,
Give thanks before embarking for more.
And as for more, that word has no end,
He who chases it, his days are already spent.
Look back and receive, look ahead in peace,
Look above and trust the omnipresence.

Embrace your lives with passionate zest,
Yet fear not death,
Death is simply a peaceful space of rest,
Like the wanderer at sunset,
Lie's in shade of serenity.

If forever was true, and nothing would end,
Life indeed would be an entrapment;
A long road without a bend,
The temporal quality of fleeting moments,
Flying past time and tide,
The joy of uncertainty,
These unchartered paths of destiny,
Mountains high, Streams downhill,
The highs and lows, the endless thrills.
Each breath you take falls into Gods plan,
The dynamic nature of time and shifting sands.

12

CONSTELLATIONS

Illuminations of the Thirtieth Light,
Cosmic ministrations,
The energy! The gravitation!
The irresistible force of a full-moon night!
Fireworks sparks, flaming kites,
Planets just born
Some silently died.
'All the world's a stage,' some day
The greatest of poets would say;
And so was the Universe
An un-orchestrated play.

Helpless between Divine games,
Maya stares at Govinda's face.
The communion tonight is strangely grave;
His eyes search her like a maze,
Smother her with anxious gaze,
Till her womb they gently embrace;
The fulcrum
Of her lonely womanhood –
An empty, aching, yearning space.

At once his mind could sense her pain,
Silently living with childlessness,
'Barren Woman' was her name.

His mind astride wild untamed stallions
Challenging boundaries, virgin hemispheres,
Unravelling the mysteries of life on earth
'Oh humanity!' he mocked,
'What are you but specks of sand,
That left your barren homes,
In search of lusher lands?
And floating on the wings of timeless time,
Found your being in your mother's womb'
That cosmos gentle, benign,
That galaxy where all matter blooms.'

A teardrop spilled from her eye,
A lonely shimmering firefly,
Instinctively his hand did rise,
Long shivering fingers gently wipe,
Soft skin singes;
The touch, a spark, electrified,
His face flushed a crimson red,

Moist body, sheathed in glistening sweat,
Her lips part, flushed in shades of bliss,
Then a quick step back from the precipice.

United in perfect synchrony,
The lovers shut their yearning eyes,
Floating images in melting shades,
Jagged visons on vaporizing screens,
Breaking embankments,
Tsunamis of passions freed.
Touched not their bodies,
Their senses embraced.

Acts of love in metaphysical ways,
Consciousness to its zenith rises,
His hands still, she feels their touch,
Emotions seething, a sensual clutch.
Like leaping flames, the two entwine,
The night oil burns, a heady wine,
Aromatic incense through senses seep,
Caressing sensations infinite, deep
His mind then sees a luminous speck,
A traveler on its final trek.

Maya shook with a splendid jolt,
Her face, her body, shone like gilded gold.
A smile spread across her face,
Caressing the miracle her womb encased,
Heart spilled with gratitude,
A Wordless promise made in solitude.
Little did they realize,
They were watched that night,
By dark, treacherous piercing eyes,
The man they called poor 'Wooden-Legs',
But more of that some other time.

13

REINCARNATION

Winter gave way to spring in time,
Season of nature's reincarnation,
Of eternal hope,
Of life.
Womb in creations spell,
Life encased in a sacred shell,
Elixirs of motherhood flow through her veins,
Flushed in peace and numbing pain,
Hands dipped in healing oils and vedic herbs,
Faithful maid and confidante,
Her soft body gently rubs.
Court soprano, a soothing note she plays
Rose drenched waters in pools of mineral clay.

Maya sensed motherhoods swell,
As the Raja stared
At her form perplexed,
His eyes on her,
Silence deep fills the air,
Broken by hesitant footsteps,

She walks to him,
A formless apparition,
Softly whispers she was with child.
'Who is the father?' he screams
'Shameless sinner!
Faithless wife!'

Her lips quiver, hands shiver,
No hopes of an explanation,
'Had she lost both sense and vision?'
His hand on its un-destined path
Did like lightning rise,
An impatient knock, before he could strike,
In the doorway stood the ageless saint,
Born with the earth said many a tale,
Himself – The ancient incarnate!

God over crown,
At his bare feet the Raja did humbly prostrate:
'Your wife has virtue.
Stands she not in a shadow of shame,
Her body holy carries an invincible soul,
An ethereal creation,

Glowing like a golden globe,
In layers of life,
Where life alone can permeate,
At the age of eight he will roam away
To become the Messiah of another day,
And he shall wait for a thousand lives,
And when hell and fire consume the world,
He will from his timelessness alight,
Savior of a tormented earth.
Give this child your protection,
– Your kind abode.'
As into the misty light,
Did his floating form submerge,
Maya like a diva glowed,
Touching the pinnacle of womanhood;
Resplendent in beauty,
And mystical motherhood.

14

CREATION

Colour pallet of the unknown painter,
Grand canvas signed, Invisible Dreamer,
Wind brushed strokes on floral bursts,
Emerald chandeliers, crystal waters,
Nature's magnificence unfurls!

The Timeless forests,
Secret vaults of geneses conserved,
The symphony, the orchestra,
Of hummingbirds,
Leaping deer in rhythmic herds,
This joyous wild,
Where life did love life,
Trickling waters, bountiful trees,
Did abound with generosities.
And when peace had come,
To all creatures wild,
Soft glow of nightfall tamed them mild,
When silence dense did prevail,
When no sound

Did that sacred moment assail,
Maya felt her body release,
The gift of life to infinity,
Govinda's child of ethereal love,
Was born.

Born to a world that would one day,
Just as the sage did say,
A million light-years away,
Plead for peace and gasp for air,
And strive for Nature, and relentlessly pray,
And he, the Lord of Nature,
Of hope,
Of life,
Would from his sanctum rise,
To save the children of another day,
Before they died silently, without a prayer.
And to the night-glow did she hold that child,
For Govinda to behold and to shelter in his eyes.
'The lords worship me, watch this sight,
I am the creator, a Goddess tonight!'

15

NEMESIS

A night of conspiracy, dark and moonless,
Hot and still with dark dreams,
Fired by darker energies;
The village men did congregate,
Desperate vigilantes
Sipping arrack, in a drunken state.

Camouflaged faces in ragged capes:
She must die! She must be slain!
Or all our dreams will be in vain!
Kill her for your ailing child!
Kill her for your mother's life!
Slay her ministrations, her deep designs,
Free once more the Healer's eyes!
'What about the physician?'
Protested one muffled voice,
'Healing is beyond cures,' he justified
The predator of the moonless night,
The man they called 'Wooden-Legs,'
'Lift up your arms, if you do agree.'

And then he smiled silently;
Watching the final seal
On his conspiracy.

16

GENESIS

The mountains stood still
Silent, divine –
Witness to the floating chariots of time,
The autumn leaves fell from their exalted place,
Mingling with Earth
In cosmic disgrace.
The holy river flowed along,
Soft nightingale sang her last summer song,
Shuffling feet dragged themselves,
Through the enchanted,
Unchanging landscape.
Her gentle face spoke of days lived and gone by,
Soft silver hair shone in fading skies.

The night was hot, the wind blew strong,
Orange dust; forebodings of a storm.

Govinda waited silently,
Restless eyes;
Shifting, impatiently searching,

Like a form in stone coming to life,
His agitation grew.
The skies had lost the glow of light,
Maya had not come tonight.
And then a commotion on the temple steps:
Maharani Ma,' cried a voice in pain,
'Our beloved queen, choked scream,
On the mountain edge, lies slain,
Will someone send a priest, for her last prayers?'

Cracking statue of alabaster-white,
Springing, moving—coming to life,
Govinda threw his head to the skies,
'Maya!' he screamed, searing the night,
'Maya! Maya!'
Echoes returned without respite,
Rising crescendo,
Ricocheting from rocks, planets
And celestial depths;
Lunging down, jaggered temple steps,
Anguished,
An injured panther in distress,
Leaping, running, a creature gone wild,

Govinda reached the Palace gates
Holding on to strong iron gates,
Let him in, this holy saint,
The Raja looked into his face,
And sensed their strangely shared fate.

Maya lay in her gilded bed,
Flower-bedecked, marigold and red
Fresh petals, roses, a resplendent headrest,
Lifeless, yet lovely,
A statue in fine ivory
Govinda, stared on mystified,
Caressing her with hallowed eyes.
'Maya,' he chanted repeatedly
That rising voice, its resounding power,
Devotional silence, now a sacred resonance,
The dying sun, new born stars,
His voice awakened the very gods
From their serenity,
'Take him away,' said a noble man,
'This poor insane priest.'
'Maya,' he chanted hypnotically,
Evoking their tryst with eternity,

'To see you, I once opened my eyes,
Today, your gaze you cannot deny.'

Bells rang through mystic heavens,
Until the sacred Mantras had woven,
Through her mortal form intrinsically,
And while all stood still, stricken, on their feet,
Maya opened her eyes.

Stunned silence, disbelief,
As the queen rose formlessly,
And like drifting leaves
In a stormy breeze,
The enchanted lovers,
Walked hand in hand,
To an unseen, waiting land,
Where gods and saints and angels dwell.

Their life was a prayer, all chants over,
The gods were quenched, their souls set free,
Freed into that sacred space,
Embraced in the realms of eternity,
All trials passed,

The cycle of birth and death silenced
Stillness, peace, and dreamless sleep...

ABOUT THE AUTHOR

Nelofar Currimbhoy shifts from prose to poetry with the ease of a natural world smith. Her first book has been translated into four languages and its Hindi version was released at the Jaipur Literature Festival.

Eyes of the Healer once again brings out her compelling talent as a story teller, this time in verse. Educated a Mater Dei Convent and Lady Shri Ram College in New Delhi, Nelofar while fulfilling a vital role in a leading company, believes in stretching the opportunity of life to experience much more, in viewing the world with curiosity and following her bliss—her love for writing. That philosophy and the journey to the spiritual self is evident in the vibrant work she has done in this book.

An active philanthropist, Nelofar runs two NGOs, Bridges Connecting Women and Bridges to Artisans, which work towards empowering woman as well as artisans and encouraging their talent. She also works closely with The Tibetan Community and imparts vocational courses to their young people.